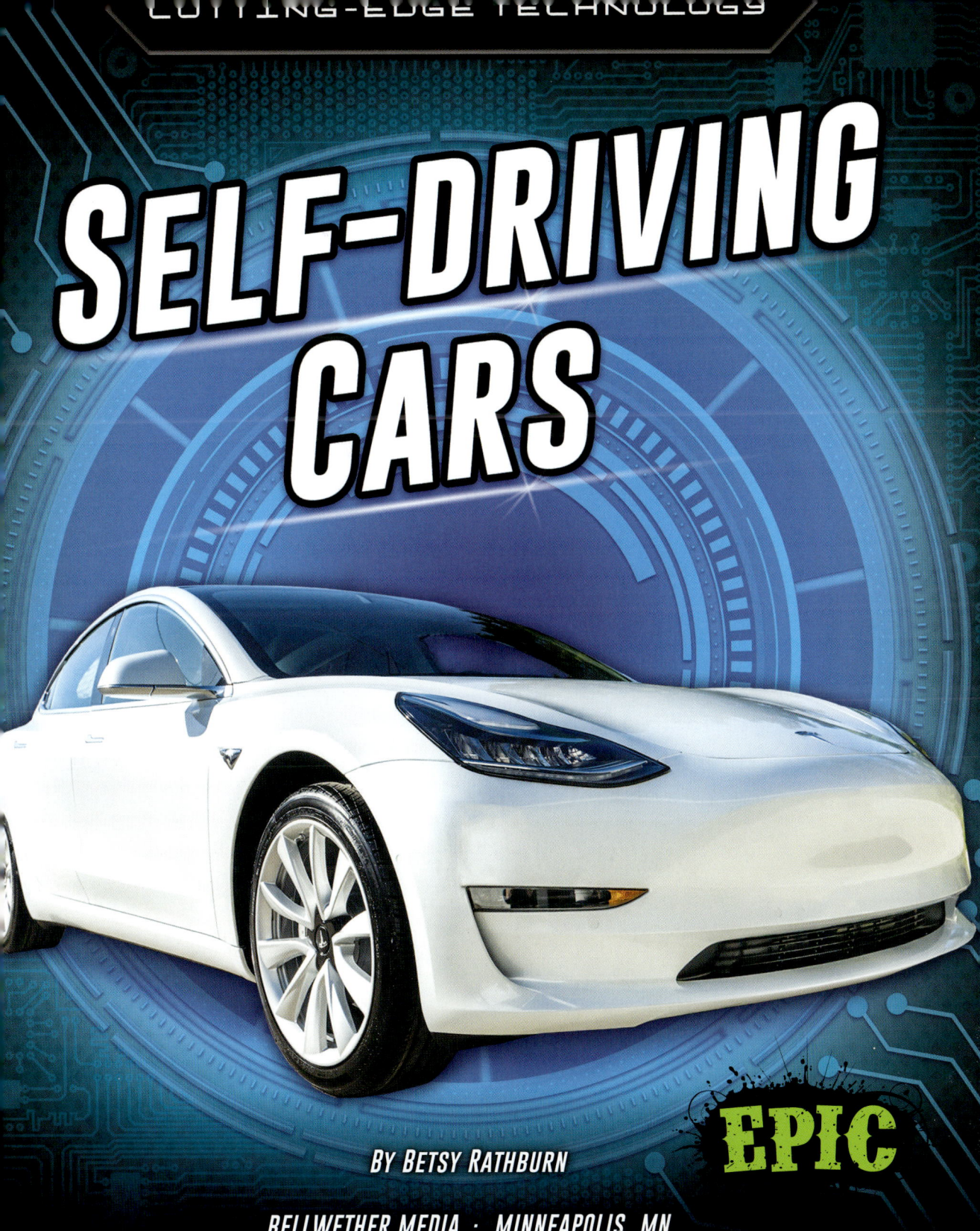

EPIC

Action and adventure collide in EPIC. Plunge into a universe of powerful beasts, hair-raising tales, and high-speed excitement. Astonishing explorations await. Can you handle it?

This edition first published in 2021 by Bellwether Media, Inc.

No part of this publication may be reproduced in whole or in part without written permission of the publisher. For information regarding permission, write to Bellwether Media, Inc., Attention: Permissions Department, 6012 Blue Circle Drive, Minnetonka, MN 55343.

Library of Congress Cataloging-in-Publication Data

LC record for Self-driving Cars available at https://lccn.loc.gov/2019059271

Text copyright © 2021 by Bellwether Media, Inc. EPIC and associated logos are trademarks and/or registered trademarks of Bellwether Media, Inc.

Editor: Kieran Downs   Designer: Josh Brink

Printed in the United States of America, North Mankato, MN.

TABLE OF CONTENTS

RUNNING LATE	4
WHAT ARE SELF-DRIVING CARS?	6
HOW THEY WORK	8
HISTORY	12
TECHNOLOGY OF TOMORROW	18
GLOSSARY	22
TO LEARN MORE	23
INDEX	24

Running Late

You are late for your flight! How will you make it on time?

A driverless van pulls up beside you. It zips across the airport. You make it to your flight. This self-driving vehicle saved the day!

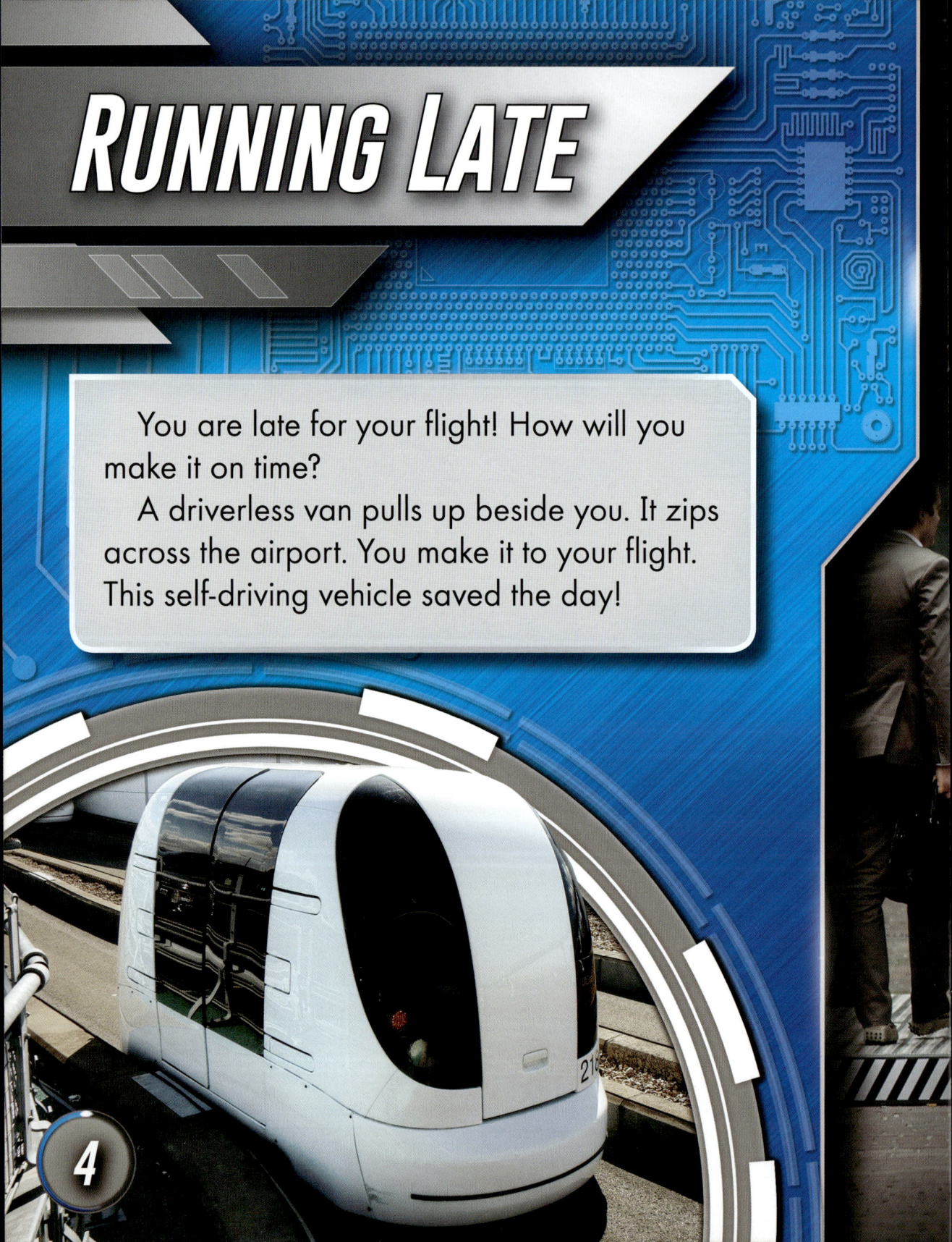

COMPANY CARS

Most people cannot buy self-driving cars yet. But companies can. The cars are used by airports and farms!

What Are Self-Driving Cars?

Self-driving cars have no drivers. Computers guide them on their **routes**.

Early Users

farmers

factories

airports

taxi services

True self-driving cars are not yet on roads. But most new cars have some self-driving features. Some can even park on their own!

How They Work

Sensors help self-driving cars drive on their own.

Lidar looks for lane markings and distances. **Radar** looks for nearby people and cars.

radar

lidar sensor

LIDAR AND RADAR

Lidar uses lasers. Radar uses invisible waves. Both measure the distance to an object!

Cameras also help see surroundings. They watch for **obstacles**. They read traffic lights and signs.

The sensors and cameras send information to a computer in the car. The computer has **software** that makes it drive like a person!

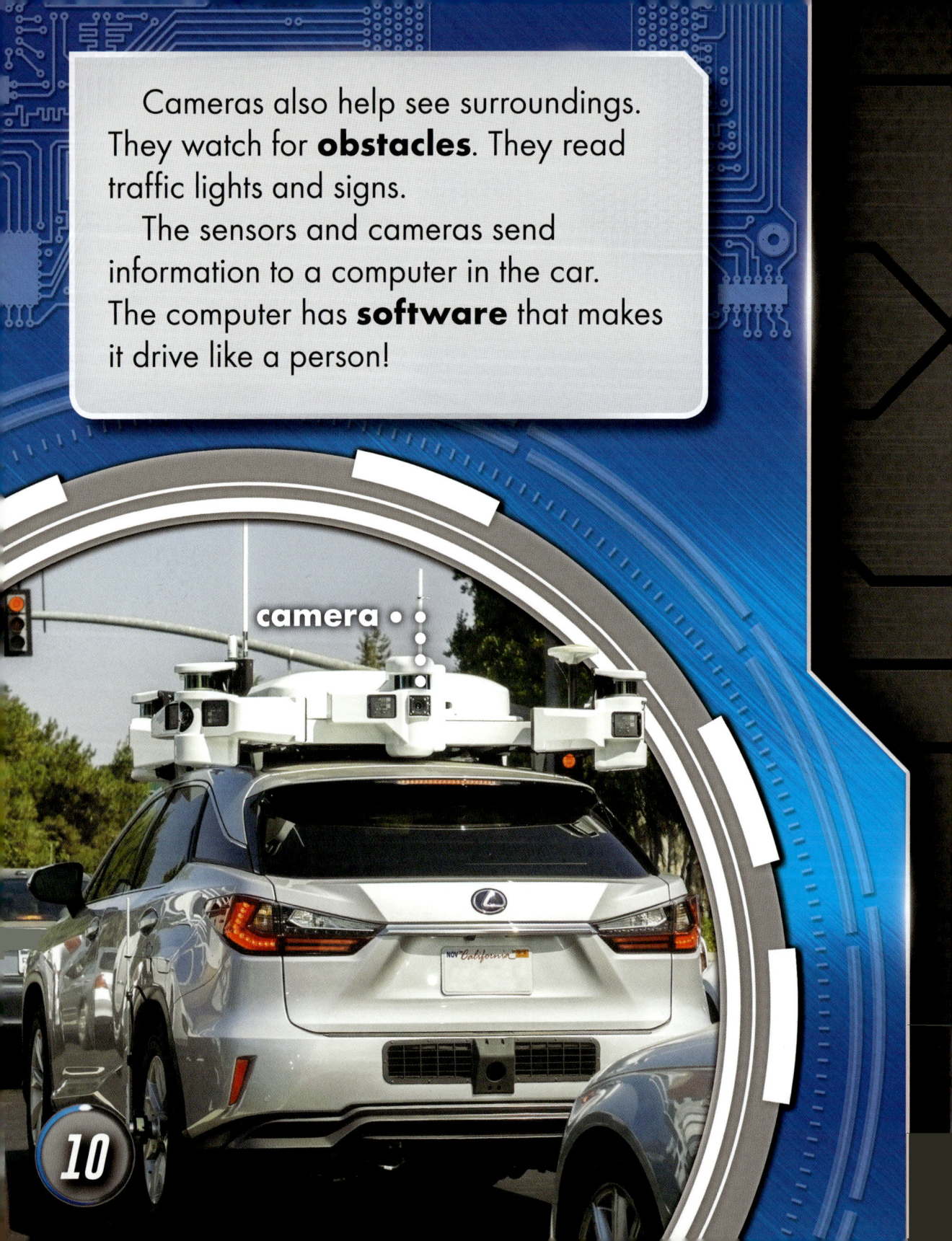

camera

How Self-driving Cars Work

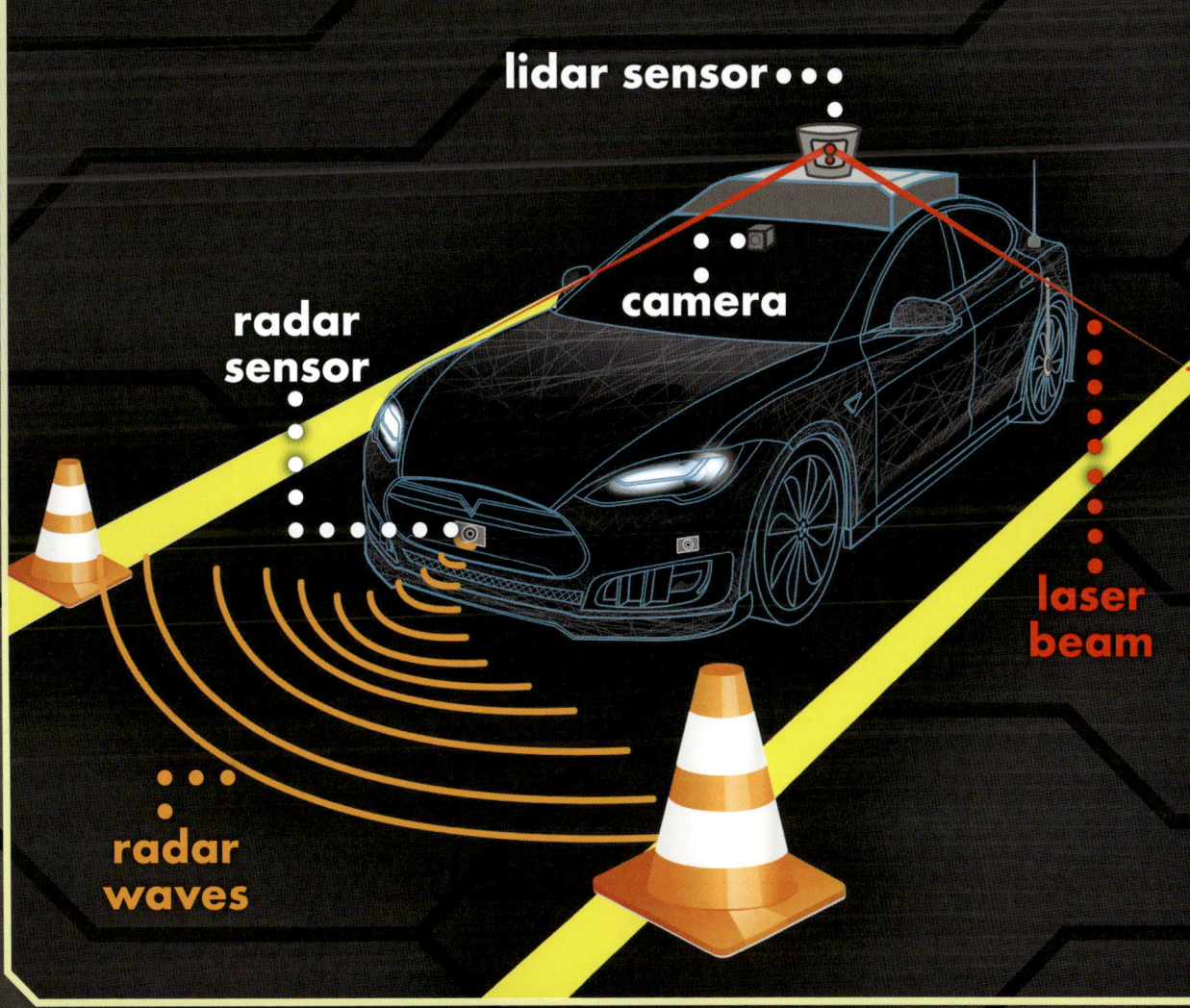

History

The first cars with computers were released in the 1960s.

That **decade** also brought the first **remote-controlled** cars. The Stanford Cart did not have a driver on board!

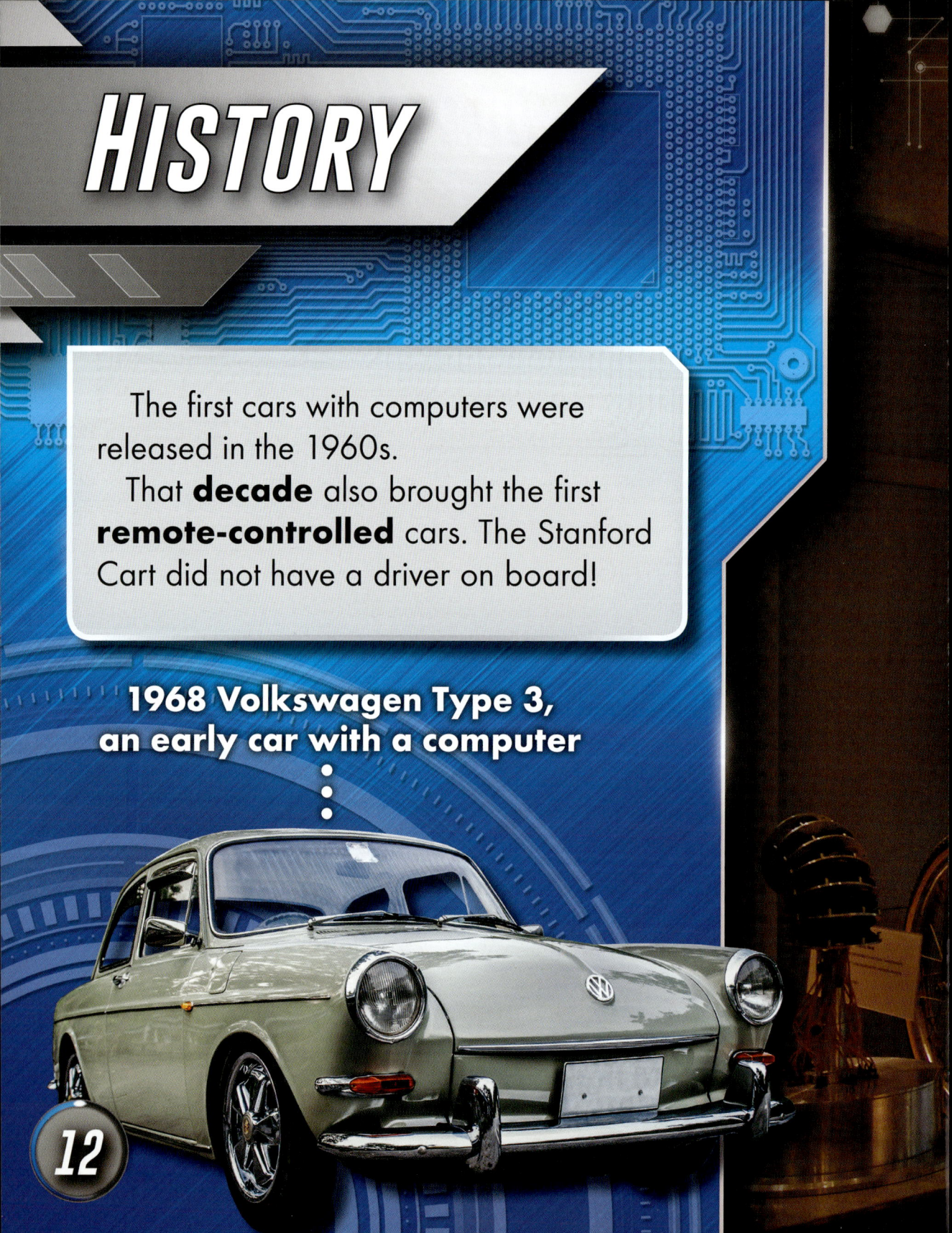

1968 Volkswagen Type 3, an early car with a computer

SLOW AND STEADY

The Stanford Cart was not fast. It moved less than 1 mile (2 kilometers) per hour!

Stanford Cart

Self-Driving Car Timeline

1960s
Researchers experiment with the Stanford Cart

1980s
Ernst Dickmanns leads the creation of the VaMoRs driverless van

1994
VaMP and VITA-2 driverless cars are introduced in Paris

Early self-driving vehicles could not drive in traffic. They were often too slow. They could not see all obstacles.

2015
Release of Tesla Autopilot lets Tesla cars steer and brake on their own

2013
New Audi A7 cars can park on their own

2017
Audi A8 Traffic Jam Pilot is released

2005
A self-driving car named Stanley wins the DARPA Grand Challenge

But in the 1990s, the VaMP and VITA-2 were introduced. These self-driving cars used cameras to drive in traffic!

The early 2000s brought more advances. The DARPA Grand Challenge offered a prize for self-driving cars. Many were created!

In 2013, a new Audi A7 was released. It could park on its own. By 2015, Tesla cars came with **autopilot**!

DARPA Grand Challenge

Go For A Ride

29 percent of people said they were very likely to ride in a self-driving car. Would you?

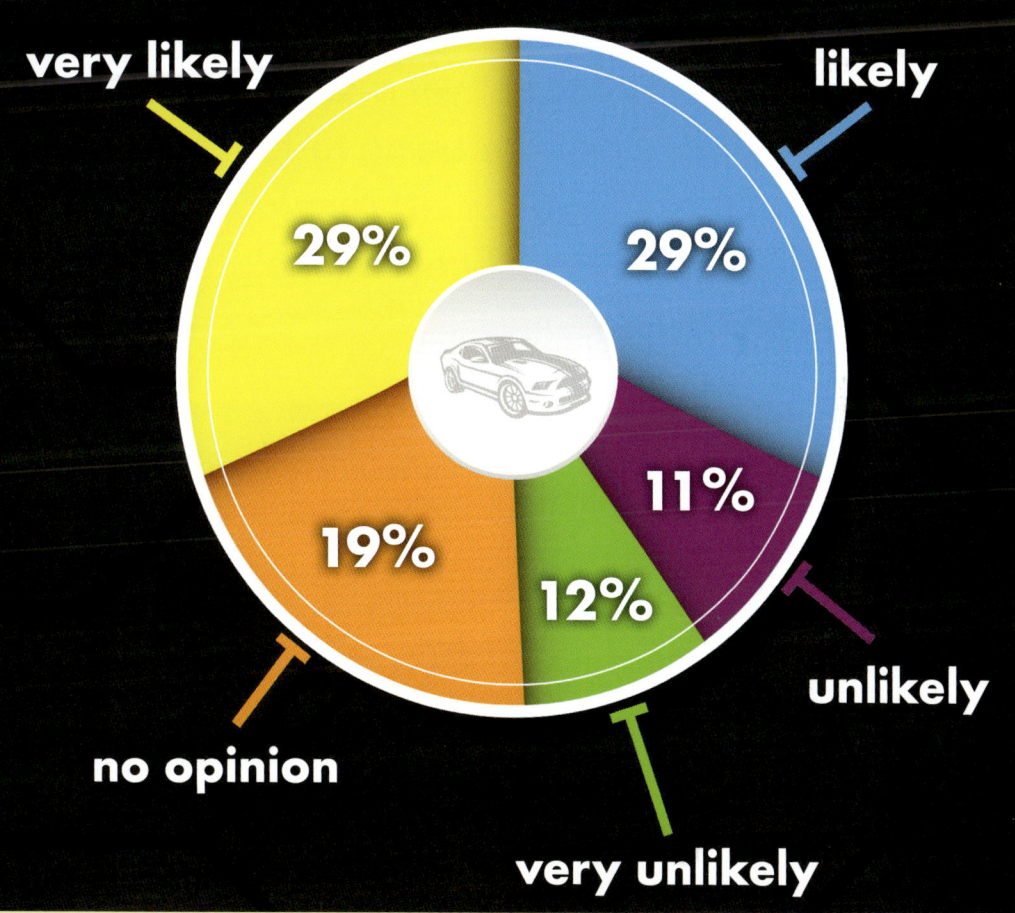

Technology of Tomorrow

Self-driving cars are not yet available to **consumers**. But they are being tested. They may make roads safer. They could cut down on traffic jams. They will help more people get around!

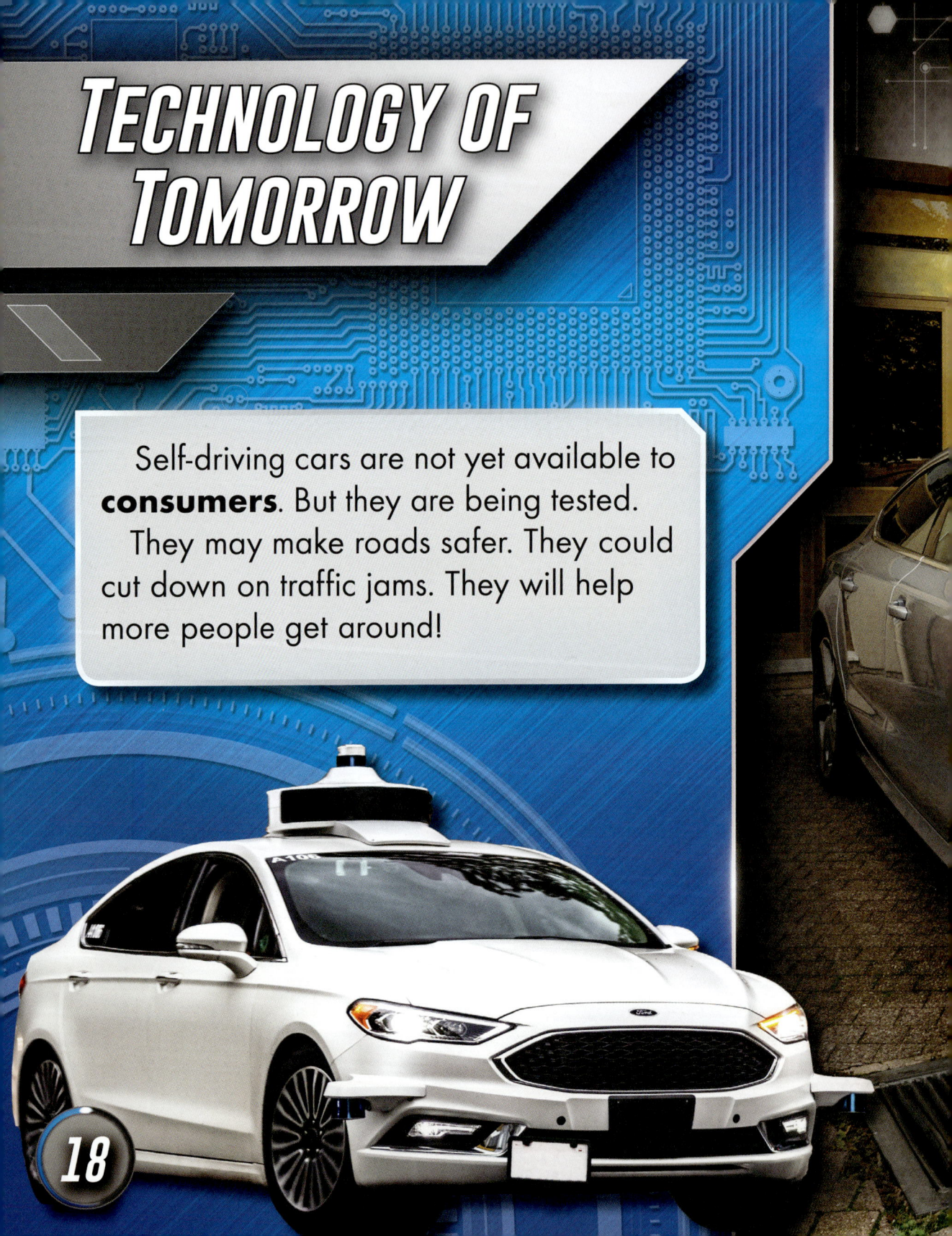

TRAFFIC JAM PILOT

In 2017, the Audi A8 was released with Traffic Jam Pilot. This let the car drive on its own at speeds up to 37 miles (60 kilometers) per hour!

Audi A8

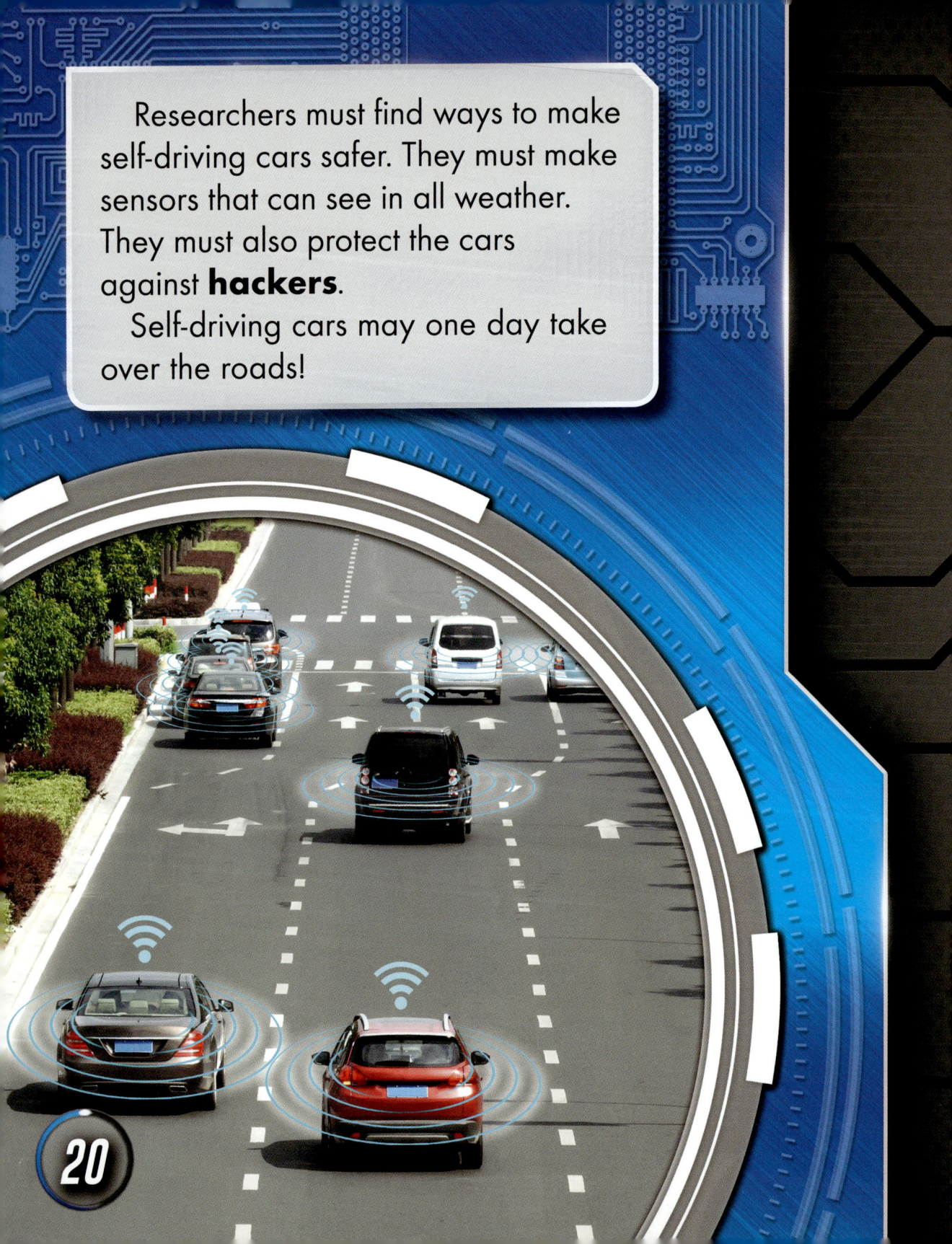

Researchers must find ways to make self-driving cars safer. They must make sensors that can see in all weather. They must also protect the cars against **hackers**.

Self-driving cars may one day take over the roads!

Pros and Cons

Pros

fewer crashes

fewer traffic jams

help people who cannot drive

Cons

could be hacked

human drivers could lose jobs

less privacy

GLOSSARY

autopilot—a software that allows a vehicle to move without a driver

consumers—people who buy things

decade—a period of ten years

hackers—people who illegally gain access to computers, often with the purpose of causing harm

lidar—a device that sends out lasers to measure distance

obstacles—things that get in the way of the movements of other things

radar—a device that sends out invisible waves to measure distance

remote-controlled—steered by a device that sends signals to the vehicle

routes—ways taken to get to other places

sensors—small devices that tell computers where something is

software—computer programs that do specific tasks

To Learn More

AT THE LIBRARY

Chandler, Matt. *The Tech Behind Self-Driving Cars*. North Mankato, Minn.: Capstone Press, 2020.

Chow-Miller, Ian. *How Self-Driving Cars Work*. New York, N.Y.: Cavendish Square, 2019.

Sonnad, Haydn. *Self-Driving Cars*. Ann Arbor, Mich.: Cherry Lake Publishing, 2019.

ON THE WEB

FACTSURFER

Factsurfer.com gives you a safe, fun way to find more information.

1. Go to www.factsurfer.com.

2. Enter "self-driving cars" into the search box and click 🔍.

3. Select your book cover to see a list of related content.

INDEX

airport, 4, 5
Audi A7, 16
Audi A8, 19
autopilot, 16
cameras, 10, 15
computers, 6, 10, 12
consumers, 18
DARPA Grand Challenge, 16
farms, 5
hackers, 20
history, 12, 13, 14, 15
how they work diagram, 11
lidar, 8, 9
obstacles, 10, 14
park, 7
pros and cons, 21
radar, 8, 9

remote-controlled cars, 12
researchers, 20
ride, 17
roads, 7, 18, 20
routes, 6
safety, 18, 20
sensors, 8, 9, 10, 20
software, 10
Stanford Cart, 12, 13
Tesla, 16
timeline, 14-15
traffic, 10, 14, 15, 18
Traffic Jam Pilot, 19
users, 5, 7
VaMP, 15
VITA-2, 15

The images in this book are reproduced through the courtesy of: TierneyMJ, cover (hero), p. 21 (top left); Dmitry Eagle Orlov, CIP; John Phillips, p. 4; Tim Jones, p. 5; Scharfsinn, p. 6; KeyWorded, p. 7 (top left); Alex Marakhovets, p. 7 (top right); THILO SCHMUELGEN, p. 7 (bottom left); Sundry Photography, pp. 7 (bottom right), 9, 18, 21 (middle left); Just_Super, p. 8; Andrei Stanescu, p. 10; sarunyu rapeearparkul, p. 12; Don DeBold, pp. 13, 14 (bottom left); Sueddeutsche Zeitung Photo, p. 14 (bottom left); Ernst D. Dickmanns, p. 14 (right); Kivaan, p. 15 (bottom left); Art Konovalov, p. 15 (middle left); EQRoy, p. 15 (top); VanderWolf Images, p. 15 (right); ZUMA Press, Inc., p. 16; Hadrian, p. 19; Zapp2Photo, p. 20; Dejan Dundjerski, p. 21 (top right); Africa Studio, p. 21 (middle right); New Africa, p. 21 (bottom left); Rawpixel.com, p. 21 (bottom right).